pub 2004 inv. 6/05
Ox  8/05

ENDANGERED AND THREATENED ANIMALS

# THE AFRICAN ELEPHANT

## A MyReportLinks.com Book

John Albert Torres

MyReportLinks.com Books

an imprint of

 Enslow Publishers, Inc. **E**

Box 398, 40 Industrial Road
Berkeley Heights, NJ 07922
USA

MyReportLinks.com Books, an imprint of Enslow Publishers, Inc. MyReportLinks®
is a registered trademark of Enslow Publishers, Inc.

**Library of Congress Cataloging-in-Publication Data**

Torres, John Albert.
  The African elephant / John Albert Torres.
     p. cm. — (Endangered and threatened animals)
  Includes bibliographical references and index.
  ISBN 0-7660-5174-9
  1. African elephant—Juvenile literature. 2. Endangered species—Juvenile literature. I. Title. II.
Series.
  QL737.P98T67 2004
  599.67′4—dc22
                                        2004003658

Printed in the United States of America

10 9 8 7 6 5 4 3 2 1

**To Our Readers:**
Through the purchase of this book, you and your library gain access to the Report Links that
specifically back up this book.
The Publisher will provide access to the Report Links that back up this book and will keep these Report
Links up to date on **www.myreportlinks.com** for three years from the book's first publication date.
We have done our best to make sure all Internet addresses in this book were active and appropriate
when we went to press. However, the author and the Publisher have no control over, and assume
no liability for, the material available on those Internet sites or on other Web sites they may link to.
The usage of the MyReportLinks.com Books Web site is subject to the terms and conditions stated
on the Usage Policy Statement on **www.myreportlinks.com**.
A password may be required to access the Report Links that back up this book. The password is
found on the bottom of page 4 of this book.
Any comments or suggestions can be sent by e-mail to comments@myreportlinks.com or to the
address on the back cover.

**Photo Credits:** AP/Wide World Photos, pp. 12, 33, 34, 43; © 1998 Takayuki Kawabe,
p. 25; © 2003 Elephant Listening Project, p. 22; © 2004 WWF—World Wildlife Fund for
Nature, pp. 21, 36; © Corel Corporation, pp. 1, 3, 10, 11, 13, 24, 26, 27, 28, 30, 32, 39,
40, 41, 44; © WWF-Canon, p. 19; John Bavaro, p. 18; MyReportLinks.com Books, p. 4;
Savanna Elephant Vocalization Project, pp. 14, 16; U.S. Fish & Wildlife Service, p. 45.

**Cover Photo:** © Corel Corporation

# Contents

# MyReportLinks.com Books
## Great Books, Great Links, Great for Research!

The Report Links listed on the following four pages can save you hours of research time by **instantly** bringing you to the best Web sites relating to your report topic.

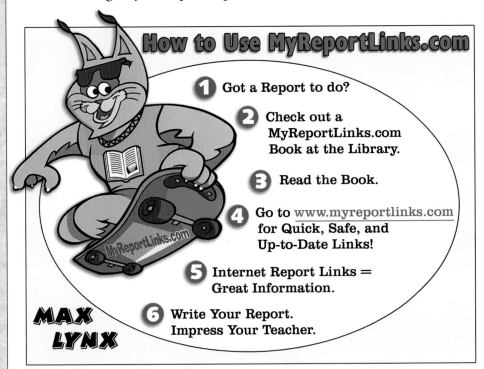

**How to Use MyReportLinks.com**

1 Got a Report to do?

2 Check out a MyReportLinks.com Book at the Library.

3 Read the Book.

4 Go to www.myreportlinks.com for Quick, Safe, and Up-to-Date Links!

5 Internet Report Links = Great Information.

6 Write Your Report. Impress Your Teacher.

**MAX LYNX**

The pre-evaluated Web sites are your links to source documents, photographs, illustrations, and maps. They also provide links to dozens—even hundreds—of Web sites about your report subject.

MyReportLinks.com Books and the MyReportLinks.com Web site save you time and make report writing easier than ever!

Please see "To Our Readers" on the copyright page for important information about this book, the MyReportLinks.com Web site, and the Report Links that back up this book. Please enter **EAE3800** if asked for a password.

## Report Links

The Internet sites described below can be accessed at
**http://www.myreportlinks.com**

▶ **The Elephants of Africa**   *EDITOR'S CHOICE

The PBS companion site to the documentary *The Elephants of Africa* includes segments on the elephant's life cycle, how the elephant uses its trunk, and how extensive the problem of poaching is.

Link to this Internet site from http://www.myreportlinks.com

▶ **Creature Feature: African Elephants**   *EDITOR'S CHOICE

*National Geographic*'s Creature Feature on the African elephant presents fun facts, a video, an audio clip, and a global elephant range map. Send an elephant postcard to a friend!

Link to this Internet site from http://www.myreportlinks.com

▶ **WWF Flagship Species: African Elephant**   *EDITOR'S CHOICE

The World Wildlife Federation's Web pages on the African elephant present extensive information on this species, including its biology, distribution, population, and threats. Conservation efforts to save the African elephant are also described.

Link to this Internet site from http://www.myreportlinks.com

▶ **African Elephant**   *EDITOR'S CHOICE

The Oakland Zoo presents information about the African elephant, including sound and video clips as well as several recorded lessons.

Link to this Internet site from http://www.myreportlinks.com

▶ **African Wildlife Foundation: Elephant**   *EDITOR'S CHOICE

The African Wildlife Foundation provides an extensive discussion of the physical characteristics, habitat, behavior, and diet of the African elephant. Trivia, a fact file, and updated links to related sites are included.

Link to this Internet site from http://www.myreportlinks.com

▶ **In the Wild: Africa—Elephant**   *EDITOR'S CHOICE

Read a good historical overview of the African elephant, its role in the ecosystem and in human society, the causes of endangerment, and conservation actions.

Link to this Internet site from http://www.myreportlinks.com

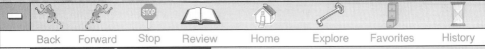
**Report Links**

The Internet sites described below can be accessed at
**http://www.myreportlinks.com**

### About African Elephants
The Toledo Zoo provides a wonderful introduction to the world of the
African elephant as well as information about breeding and conservation
of elephants in the wild.

*Link to this Internet site from http://www.myreportlinks.com*

### The African Elephant
Vital statistics and information about the African elephant's diet, society,
and ways of communication can be found at this site. Conservation efforts
to save the elephants are also discussed.

*Link to this Internet site from http://www.myreportlinks.com*

### African Elephant Bibliography
You can search annotated bibliographies of more than forty-two hundred
titles spanning the biology, ecology, and management of the African elephant.
Guidelines for requesting copies of the referenced material are provided.

*Link to this Internet site from http://www.myreportlinks.com*

### African Elephant Conservation Trust
Learn about the African Elephant Conservation Trust at its Web site.
See how you can help save the African elephant from extinction.

*Link to this Internet site from http://www.myreportlinks.com*

### African Elephant Picture Gallery
Look at a portfolio of photographs of African Elephants in the wild taken at
the Tembe National Park on the South Africa/Mozambique border. You can
access a live Webcam, too!

*Link to this Internet site from http://www.myreportlinks.com*

### The African Elephant Specialist Group
An excellent source for research on African elephant populations, the AfESG site
includes the African Elephant Database as well as African elephant status reports.

*Link to this Internet site from http://www.myreportlinks.com*

**Report Links**

 The Internet sites described below can be accessed at
### http://www.myreportlinks.com

▶**African Elephants**
Ahali Elephants is a nonprofit organization that identifies, monitors, and assists captive elephants living alone or in inadequate conditions in North America. The site provides a look at their work.

Link to this Internet site from http://www.myreportlinks.com

▶**Animal Bytes: Elephant**
Animal Bytes provides a comparison between African and Asian elephants as well as many facts about each of these majestic mammals.

Link to this Internet site from http://www.myreportlinks.com

▶**CITES**
CITES is an international agreement between governments whose aim is to ensure that international trade in wild animals and plants does not threaten their survival. This site documents CITES' efforts to protect the African elephant and other species.

Link to this Internet site from http://www.myreportlinks.com

▶**Echo of the Elephants: The Next Generation**
PBS presents field work, research, and information on elephants in Amboseli, including the elephants' communication methods.

Link to this Internet site from http://www.myreportlinks.com

▶**Elephant**
MSN Encarta's encyclopedia entry on the elephant includes an extensive discussion of the elephant's evolution, range, habitat, diet, reproduction, behavior, intelligence, and relationship with humans.

Link to this Internet site from http://www.myreportlinks.com

▶**Elephant, Loxodonta Africana**
This site provides a very thorough discussion of the African elephant's range, ecology, social and mating system, offspring and maternal care, communications, and behavior.

Link to this Internet site from http://www.myreportlinks.com

 The Internet sites described below can be accessed at
**http://www.myreportlinks.com**

▶ **Elephant Information Repository**
Check out this comprehensive database about elephants. It includes information about elephant family structure, anatomy, senses, life cycle, threats, and much more.

Link to this Internet site from http://www.myreportlinks.com

▶ **The Elephant Listening Project**
The Elephant Listening Project monitors African forest elephant populations using bioacoustics rather than the more common method of counting dung piles. Bioacoustics uses sensors to listen to elephants when they make noises such as roars and grunts.

Link to this Internet site from http://www.myreportlinks.com

▶ **The Elephant Men**
This is the companion site to PBS's documentary on the Elephant Men, the people who train and work with elephants. Included is a discussion of peaceful coexistence between the elephant and man, as well as a comparison between African and Asian elephants.

Link to this Internet site from http://www.myreportlinks.com

▶ **Elephant Research in Mozambique**
This site describes and tracks the research efforts being undertaken at the Maputo Elephant Reserve in southern Mozambique. Includes a discussion of research findings.

Link to this Internet site from http://www.myreportlinks.com

▶ **Elephants in Addo Elephant National Park**
View pictures of wild African elephants from Addo Elephant National Park in South Africa. See elephants bathing, alone, in herds, and as families.

Link to this Internet site from http://www.myreportlinks.com

▶ **The Elephants of Cameroon**
This site, sponsored by Field Trip Earth, documents progress relating to Cameroon's National Elephant Management Plan. This site includes articles about African elephants, information about the project and the region, research data, and a media gallery.

Link to this Internet site from http://www.myreportlinks.com

## Report Links

The Internet sites described below can be accessed at
**http://www.myreportlinks.com**

▶ **Encyclopedia.com: Elephant**
This research article from Encyclopedia.com presents an overview
of the elephant, a comparison between African and Asian elephants,
a discussion of the relationship between elephants and humans,
and more.

Link to this Internet site from http://www.myreportlinks.com

▶ **Introduction to Elephant Country**
This site was designed to create awareness and support for elephant
conservation efforts through information, pictures, audio clips, songs,
quotes, and much more.

Link to this Internet site from http://www.myreportlinks.com

▶ **Introduction to the Proboscidea**
This site from UC Berkeley provides an introduction to the elephant's
living relatives. Only two species of elephant survive.

Link to this Internet site from http://www.myreportlinks.com

▶ **Living With Elephants**
Living With Elephants is a foundation dedicated to the exploration of
the relationship between African elephants and people. Their "Monthly
Field Notes" are especially fascinating.

Link to this Internet site from http://www.myreportlinks.com

▶ **Savanna Elephant Vocalization Project**
Access material from years of field studies relating to elephant voices
and communication. Learn why, how, and what elephants communicate.

Link to this Internet site from http://www.myreportlinks.com

▶ **Save the Elephants**
Save the Elephants (STE) is a leading organization approaching
conservation from the elephant's point of view. STE's site presents
a ton of information on elephants and their conservation.

Link to this Internet site from http://www.myreportlinks.com

## African Elephant Facts

▷ **Class**
Mammalia

▷ **Family**
Elephantidae

▷ **Genus**
*Loxodonta*

▷ **Species**
*Africana*

▷ **Average Height***
Male: 11 feet (3.4 meters)
Female: 9 feet (2.8 meters)

▷ **Average Weight**
Male: 12,000 pounds
(5,443 kilograms)
Female: 8,000 pounds
(3,629 kilograms)

▷ **Life Span**
About 65 years

▷ **Status**
Threatened

▷ **Skin Color**
Dark gray

▷ **Gestation Period**
22 months

▷ **Offspring**
One every four to five years

▷ **Range**
Africa—Mainly the Savannas,
forests, and river valleys of
Central Africa.

▷ **Travel Speed**
Average speed is 3 to 6 miles
per hour (4.8 to 9.7 kilometers per hour).
Maximum speed is about 25
miles per hour (40.2 kilometers per hour).

▷ **Tusk Length**
Up to 8 feet (2.4 meters)

▷ **Threats to Survival**
Poachers, habitat loss

▷ **Voice**
Elephants can make rumbling
sounds, screams, roars, bel-
lows, groans, and squeaks.

▷ **Water**
Elephants are fond of the
water, and are very good
swimmers.

*All metric measurements in this book are estimates.*

# An Illegal Slaughter

**T**he shots echoed through the African forests. Rangers hired to stop elephant poachers were scrambling to follow the noise of the gun blasts. They jumped in their jeeps while others climbed aboard a helicopter. They grabbed their guns in hopes that they could catch the poachers. Often, they know they will get there too late. Their only hope is that somehow the poachers will have left a trail for the rangers to follow. Even this, though, is doubtful.

The rangers can only follow the circling vultures to where the shootings took place. By the time they arrive,

▲ An African elephant in the grassland. Elephants are the heaviest land animals in the world.

▲ *David Western, the Kenya Wildlife Service director, looks at the remains of a poached elephant. The tusks have been removed.*

they find a sickening sight. A pregnant elephant has been shot and killed, her sprawling body and unborn baby left to rot in the 90°F (32°C) temperatures. The elephant's head has been brutally massacred so that poachers could remove her long ivory tusks—a poacher's prize.

Poachers are people that illegally kill or steal animals to sell them or use them for profit. They have begun to hunt the smaller African elephants of the forests. They have already nearly wiped out the larger elephants of the savannas and plains.

Elephants are the heaviest land animal in the world as well as the second tallest. Some people call elephants the true king of the beasts. Elephants have no natural enemies. They walk the savanna plains and thick African forests fearing no predator. Once in a while, lions may try to attack a baby elephant, but even this is rare. The elephants' sheer size and strength alone can deter any other animal from attacking. Between 1979 and 1989, however, African elephants began vanishing from the African plains and forests at an alarming rate. It seems the elephants' worst enemy is people's desire to have their beautiful ivory tusks. Because of the worldwide demand for ivory—what elephant tusks are made of—elephants were being slaughtered illegally so that poachers could hack off the prized tusks and sell them on the black market (illegally).

## The Appeal of Ivory

Ivory has been used to help make jewelry, sculptures, piano keys, and tools. Tusks start out as long, curved incisor teeth in elephants' mouths. These teeth then continue to grow,

▲ A mother and baby elephant are out for a walk. The mother's tusks are fully formed, and even her youngster's tusks have begun to come in.

sometimes reaching 8 feet (2.4 meters) long and weighing up to 150 pounds (68 kilograms) each! Almost everyone at some point has touched something made of ivory.

African governments have cracked down on poaching and made killing elephants illegal. Still, many poachers risk death by killing these gigantic beasts for their tusks. It was thought by many that the African Elephant Conservation Act of 1988, which banned the trade of ivory in the United States, would help save the elephants from becoming extinct. Yet it appears much more than a law will be needed to stop the poaching.

The African elephant, one of the most majestic and clearly the most recognizable animals in the world, is

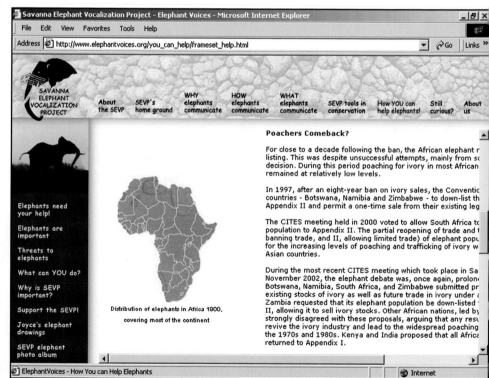

The orange portion of this map of the African continent shows where elephants could be found in 1900.

endangered. The only thing that can save the beautiful giants are humans—the same species that threatens to move the animal closer to extinction. A species becomes extinct when there are no more animals of that type. For example, dinosaurs are extinct because there are none left.

## An Alarming Sight

In fact, in September 1996, during a time when African leaders thought they had poaching under control, something disastrous was discovered.

Michael Fay is an elephant researcher with the Wildlife Conservation Society. Based in the Bronx, New York, the Wildlife Conservation Society works globally to save wildlife and wild lands. Fay was flying his small airplane over a remote clearing just outside the Nouabale-Ndoki National Park in the northern Congo when he spotted some dead elephants. Little did he know the extent of the needless slaughter. Fay was unable to land there in his plane, so he returned the following day in a helicopter and with some television reporters.

They found more than three hundred dead elephants—all killed by poachers. There were even baby elephants among the dead. Two months later, Fay's worst nightmare would come true when he found more than one thousand dead elephants near the same spot.

Fay was outraged. Along with some friends, he personally chased the poachers from the area by destroying their camp over and over again and harassing them until they left. By the following spring, illegal poaching in that area had stopped. Fay never wanted to see a dead elephant, killed for its tusks, ever again.[1]

The numbers detailing the decline of the African elephant are scary. In 1977, researchers say there were more than

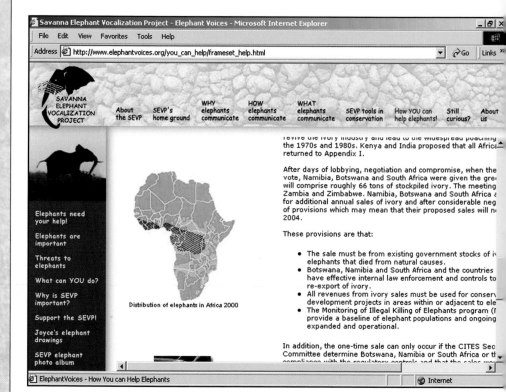

Savanna Elephant Vocalization Project - Elephant Voices - Microsoft Internet Explorer

File  Edit  View  Favorites  Tools  Help

Address http://www.elephantvoices.org/you_can_help/frameset_help.html    Go   Links

SAVANNA ELEPHANT VOCALIZATION PROJECT

About the SEVP   SEVP's home ground   WHY elephants communicate   HOW elephants communicate   WHAT elephants communicate   SEVP tools in conservation   How YOU can help elephants!   Still curious?   About us

Elephants need your help!

Elephants are important

Threats to elephants

What can YOU do?

Why is SEVP important?

Support the SEVP!

Joyce's elephant drawings

SEVP elephant photo album

Distribution of elephants in Africa 2000

revive the ivory industry and lead to the widespread poaching
the 1970s and 1980s. Kenya and India proposed that all Africa
returned to Appendix I.

After days of lobbying, negotiation and compromise, when the
vote, Namibia, Botswana and South Africa were given the gre
will comprise roughly 66 tons of stockpiled ivory. The meeting
Zambia and Zimbabwe. Namibia, Botswana and South Africa a
for additional annual sales of ivory and after considerable neg
of provisions which may mean that their proposed sales will n
2004.

These provisions are that:

- The sale must be from existing government stocks of iv
  elephants that died from natural causes.
- Botswana, Namibia and South Africa and the countries
  have effective internal law enforcement and controls to
  re-export of ivory.
- All revenues from ivory sales must be used for conser
  development projects in areas within or adjacent to ele
- The Monitoring of Illegal Killing of Elephants program (I
  provide a baseline of elephant populations and ongoing
  expanded and operational.

In addition, the one-time sale can only occur if the CITES Sec
Committee determine Botswana, Namibia or South Africa or th

ElephantVoices - How You can Help Elephants                    Internet

▲ This is the same map of Africa showing where elephants could be found in the year 2000. Both the number of elephants and their range have shrunk considerably in the last one hundred years.

1.3 million elephants in Africa. By 1997, only twenty years later, there were only six hundred thousand left. If that pace were maintained, then there would not be any more African elephants by the year 2017.

## ▶ Efforts at Conservation

In recent years, efforts to save the elephants have gained momentum. Elephant parks have been built throughout Africa to try and save the beasts. Huge pieces of land have been put aside in many countries where the elephants are strongly protected. The hope is that the animals will start having babies and once again have a population in the millions. Africa is not alone in this battle to save the elephant. There are many active organizations in several countries including the United States, Germany, England, and Sweden that raise money and awareness to try and save the gentle giants.

Kenya is one of the African countries where elephants live. The government of Kenya decided to show poachers and the world in general that killing elephants for their ivory would be unacceptable. The Kenyans were hoping that other nations with elephants would take notice. The government had taken millions of dollars worth of tusks from poachers they had captured. Then, with television cameras rolling, they set the treasure on fire to make it worthless.

Some people said they should have sold the ivory and used the money to help protect the elephants, but the government leaders did not agree. They thought it would be better to show the world that no ivory sales would be allowed.

To save the African elephant from extinction, it will take a worldwide effort by people who care about this majestic beast. The question now is "can people help the elephant survive?"

# Chapter 2

# Special Characteristics

**E**lephants are probably the most recognizable animal in the world. Just about everyone can picture these gray giants with their long trunks, big flapping ears, and long white tusks. The elephants are very specialized animals, and their unique features all have a special purpose.

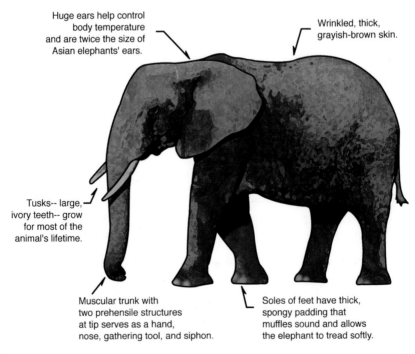

Huge ears help control body temperature and are twice the size of Asian elephants' ears.

Wrinkled, thick, grayish-brown skin.

Tusks-- large, ivory teeth-- grow for most of the animal's lifetime.

Muscular trunk with two prehensile structures at tip serves as a hand, nose, gathering tool, and siphon.

Soles of feet have thick, spongy padding that muffles sound and allows the elephant to tread softly.

▲ *A drawing of an African elephant. These elephants differ slightly from the Indian elephants that can be found in parts of Asia.*

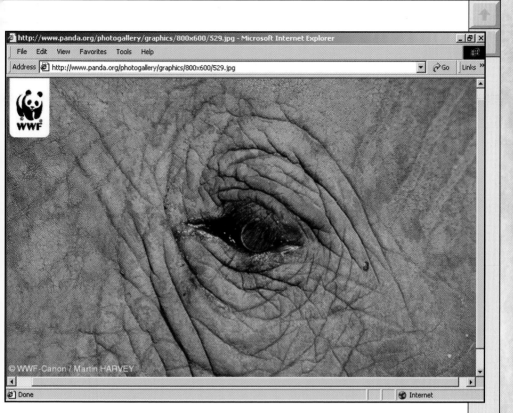

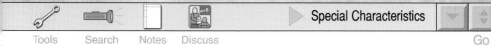

Although they have pretty large eyes, elephants do not have very good eyesight. They mostly rely on their excellent sense of smell.

## ▷ The Largest Land Animal

The first and most notable characteristic of the elephant is its great size. Male African elephants weigh up to 13,200 pounds (5,987 kilograms) and can grow up to 11 feet (3.4 meters) high. Females are slightly smaller, reaching 7,700 pounds (3,493 kilograms) and nearly 8.5 feet (2.6 meters) tall.

There are also forest elephants living in Africa. These animals have developed smaller bodies to be able to move freely in the dense, thick forests. These animals are typically 9 feet (2.7 meters) tall and weigh about 5,000 pounds (2,268 kilograms).

Another interesting difference between the larger African savanna—or plains elephant—and its cousins in the forest is in their number of toes. Savanna elephants have four toes on their front feet and three on their rear feet. Forest elephants have five toes in the front and four in the back.

## Elephant Ears

The ears of an elephant distinguish it from all other animals. An African elephant's ears measure about four feet (1.2 meters) across. These ears, while used for hearing, can also be used by the animal to cool itself. It does this by flapping its ears back and forth.

Elephants can also use their ears to communicate with one another. For example, an elephant will level its ears down when it is feeling shy or submissive, much like a dog. An angry elephant will flare its ears out wildly to look bigger than it really is.

## The Trunk

Probably the most unique looking and most interesting part of an elephant is its trunk. The trunk of an adult African elephant is about seven feet (2.1 meters) long. It is really just a long nose and upper lip attached together.

Elephants use their trunks to smell things, the way most animals use their noses. These long boneless flexible trunks, though, are used for much more than smelling.

In fact, elephant trunks have two fingerlike points on the tip of their trunk that allow elephants to gently pick up the smallest of objects, such as a berry from a tree. They can also be used to grasp thick objects such as a tree branch. The trunk is so strong that it is capable of lifting objects that weigh up to 600 pounds (272.2 kilograms).

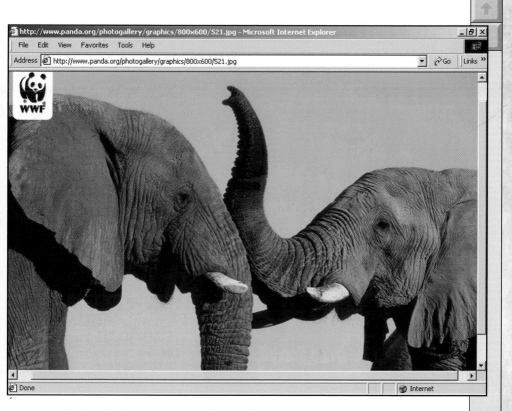

http://www.panda.org/photogallery/graphics/800x600/521.jpg - Microsoft Internet Explorer

File   Edit   View   Favorites   Tools   Help

Address   http://www.panda.org/photogallery/graphics/800x600/521.jpg    ⮎Go   Links »

Done      Internet

▲ *Elephants use can use their trunks to communicate, among many other things. The elephants pictured here are greeting one another.*

       Elephants also use their trunks to touch and comfort one another—another form of communication. It is common to see mother elephants caressing their babies with their trunks.

       One of the most unique things an elephant can do with its trunk is to use it like a hose when it is thirsty. It also does this to give itself a shower. An elephant can pull up to about one and a half gallons (six liters) of water into its trunk at one time. Then it bends its trunk under and puts the tip of the trunk into its mouth. Then it blows, pumping the water into its mouth, right down its throat.

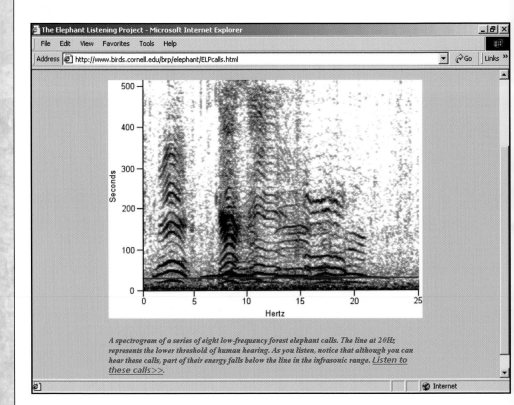

The Elephant Listening Project - Microsoft Internet Explorer

File    Edit    View    Favorites    Tools    Help

Address http://www.birds.cornell.edu/brp/elephant/ELPcalls.html

*A spectrogram of a series of eight low-frequency forest elephant calls. The line at 20Hz represents the lower threshold of human hearing. As you listen, notice that although you can hear these calls, part of their energy falls below the line in the infrasonic range. Listen to these calls>>.*

Internet

▲ This chart shows the frequency of elephant calls. Elephant ears can pick up sounds that the human ear can not.

In many parts of Africa, the sun raises the temperature until it is blazing hot. As a result, elephants sometimes need to cover their bodies in mud. The mud works as a sunscreen. Here, once again, the trunk is used to do this. First the elephant uses its trunk to spray cool water over its body. Then it uses its trunk to spray sand or dirt onto its back. The layer of dirt mixes with the water to create a mud pack on the elephant's body.

Another use for these amazing trunks is that elephants use them when they are swimming underwater. An elephant can use its trunk as a snorkel. It can keep the tip of the trunk above the water, which allows the animal to breathe while it swims.

Elephants also use their trunks for talking. They can make loud trumpeting noises, usually as a warning to other elephants or to scare off a pride of lions.

## ▶ Diet

Being such a large animal, elephants spend a lot of time eating. In fact, elephants spend about sixteen hours a day eating. Their diet consists of things like grass, leaves, twigs, bark, and fruit. Some of their favorite foods include cattails and papyrus. During their sixteen-hour dinners, elephants consume between 200 and 600 pounds (91 and 272 kilograms) of food. Of course, with all that food comes the need for drink. Elephants are capable of drinking 60 gallons (227 liters) of water a day. Elephants can only digest half of what they eat. As a result, each elephant must eat twice what it actually needs.

## ▶ Social Lives of Elephants

Another important trait for elephant life is the fact that it is a matriarchal animal. This means that elephants travel in small herds ruled by the oldest female. She will let elephants in her herd know when it is time to eat or drink, rest or bathe.

Female elephants all stick together and play an active role in raising the young elephants as well. Every female acts as a mother to a baby in the herd. The male elephants, once they are old enough to mate, often go off alone. They will spend the rest of their lives meeting different herds of elephants, spending some time with them and then moving on.

Elephants are very specialized animals that have intricate social lives, ranging from forming elephant graveyards to

Elephants travel in small herds ruled by the oldest female.

showing respect to the oldest female in the herd.[1] Elephants can exhibit extreme strength in ripping up a forest, yet they can move a small tortoise gently aside with their leg so that it will not get smashed. They can scare off a group of hungry hyenas, yet they tend to their young with incredible amounts of love and affection.

## Chapter 3 ▶

# Habitat Destruction and Other Threats

**T**here is no doubt that habitat destruction has put the African elephant in a perilous state. As the elephants continue to lose land they must go closer and closer to farms or other places where there are people to find food. It is also true that the elephant does a lot of destruction to its own habitat.

http://www2.jan.ne.jp/~kawabe/addo/img/el_cld0s.jpg - Microsoft Internet Explorer

File    Edit    View    Favorites    Tools    Help

Address http://www2.jan.ne.jp/~kawabe/addo/img/el_cld0s.jpg    Go    Links »

Done                                                    Internet

▲ *Elephants dig to create water holes that they can drink from or bathe in. Mud bathing helps elephants keep cool because the mud blocks some of the rays from the hot sun.*

## ▷ Naturally Clearing the Land

You can always tell when a herd of elephants has been through an area simply by viewing the scenes of massive destruction. There are long and wide areas of trampled, dug-up land, hundreds and thousands of trees pulled-out by the roots, and huge craters in the ground where elephants decided to dig for mineral deposits in the soil. The elephants pack down the soil so hard that it can actually lead to erosion. Erosion occurs when the soil gets worn away.

On the other hand, elephants do as much good for the environment as bad. Indeed, it has been said that Africa would look a whole lot different if there were no elephants. There is plenty of good that comes from the elephants' destruction. They can turn wooded or forested areas into grasslands, which is good for savanna animals that need

▲ As they walk around, elephants clear the land around them. This elephant is moving forward. Not much can stand in its path.

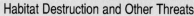

▲ *As elephants walk, they stir up insects from the ground. The birds that live in the habitat feed on these insects.*

grasses to graze on. Elephants also create water holes by digging in dry riverbeds. They coat themselves with mud from the water's edge, which helps create larger watering holes. Elephants also create caves when they start digging into the sides of rock looking for salts. These caves get used by other animals looking for shelter.

When elephants walk, they also help the bird world by stirring up insects that the birds eat. In addition, elephants help spread plants and species to other areas when they pass seeds through their bodies. In fact, one plant—the African eggplant—grows only after it has been passed through the elephant's stomach and fertilized by the animal's dung.

Actually, many types of trees spring right from seeds that are deposited on the ground inside the elephant's

▲ *This male Indian elephant is taking a mud bath. Indian elephants and African elephants have some differences. Indian elephants are the ones usually used by a traveling circus.*

dung. Baboons will also help new trees form when they accidentally spread seeds in the elephant's dung as they forage for insects. Dung beetles get their name because they lay their eggs in elephant droppings.

When elephants knock over trees or destroy them while they eat, they open a hole in the forest canopy, or ceiling. This allows more sunlight than normal to shine through. In the fertile African forests this means new plants will take root. These plants then become food for smaller herbivores (plant eaters) that share the same feeding grounds as the majestic elephants.

## Logging

It is clear that the elephant does as much good as it does bad regarding the forests and grassy plains where it lives. Logging, however, is another form of habitat destruction that is of no benefit to the land. Logging is the process of cutting down trees in order to sell the wood, called lumber. Logging does almost as much damage to the elephant population as poachers looking for ivory.

Logging, especially in Africa's Congo Basin, is putting forest elephants as well as several other types of animals in severe danger. The forests of the Congo are the second largest rain forest in the world after the Amazon rain forest. The Congo Basin forests cover 470 million acres (1.9 million square kilometers) of land. Machinery used by loggers, such as chain saws, can destroy a forest very quickly. In fact, the World Wildlife Federation claims that nearly 10 million acres (40,468 square kilometers) of forest are logged every year. That means by the year 2040, 70 percent of the forest could be gone. While this obviously threatens survival of the elephants, it also endangers hundreds of other types of animals that live or feed in the thick, lush forests.

▲ Habitat destruction causes elephants to have to migrate farther and farther for food. The elephant shown here is feeding in a swamp.

Even though the logging is illegal, it continues, and loggers—just like poachers—are very hard to catch. The loggers create roads for their vehicles to haul the fallen trees out of the forests. This helps poachers because poachers can then use these roads to gain access into the forests that they could never reach before. Some animals such as chimpanzees, lowland gorillas, and forest elephants have already vanished from certain parts of the forests, making them locally extinct from areas they were always known to be. There are already parts of Africa that no longer have elephants. It is a terrible loss.

## ▶ Similar Problems in Asia

The African elephant's cousin, the Indian elephant, is also in grave danger because of logging and habitat destruction of one of its major homes—the Tesso Nilo Forest in

Indonesia. In Asia, the smaller elephants have been used for hundreds of years as beasts of burden or transportation. African elephants cannot be tamed enough to be used. That is why 90 percent of the elephants you see in circuses or animal shows are the Indian elephants.

The obvious main problem of habitat destruction is that elephants are big animals that need a lot of vegetation to eat in order to survive. The more land that is used by people, the less land there is for elephants. When elephants are forced onto reserves or national parks in order to save them from poachers, they often run out of food quickly. Some elephants have even starved to death. It becomes a vicious cycle because the hungry elephants start to migrate and often go right where the poachers are waiting.

## Big Eaters

Sometimes elephants can eat for up to twenty hours a day. Because they have to eat so much, they mainly eat while they walk. Elephants though, are quick for their size and can reach speeds of up to 15 miles (24 kilometers) per hour. They can actually walk about fifty miles (eighty kilometers) in a single day.

Despite habitat destruction and the loss of much of their lands, the gentle creature's biggest threat remains the poachers. Many of the African countries are very poor. People will risk their lives and the extinction of elephants in order to take ivory tusks from the elephants. Even with the strict laws banning ivory sales, more than 80 percent of the world's ivory comes from illegally killed elephants.

**Chapter 4 ▶**

# Growing Concern

**T**he demand for ivory products made from elephant tusks has put the gentle giants at great risk of extinction.

## ▷ History of the Ivory Trade

The ivory trade is not new. It has existed for a very long time, some say about twenty-seven thousand years. Many artists throughout the world have made fortunes by carving intricate, beautiful scenes onto ivory. Unfortunately, the only way to get ivory from an elephant is to kill it. For thousands of years, artists in the Orient have carved designs on the ivory

△ *A baby elephant calf takes a rest while other elephants are beside it.*

*African countries are hiring anti-poaching troopers to try to stop ivory poaching. This trooper came too close to a baby elephant and now the angry mother is charging at him.*

tusks. In Japan, the ivory is used to make something called "hankas." These are special seals that each family has. In other Asian countries such as China, the ancient art of carving is a vital industry. Carving businesses are often passed down in families from generation to generation. In Western countries people seek items made of ivory for souvenirs. The demand for these items threatens the survival of the elephant, the largest land mammal on earth.

Poaching elephants for the ivory trade has been going on for a very long time. In 1903, elephants nearly became extinct in South Africa. Then, the poachers began moving north to find more and more elephants to kill.

## Banning the Ivory Trade

The year 1989 served as a wake-up call. The actions taken that year may be what ultimately saves the elephants from extinction. That is the year that conservation experts and people who studied elephants said the animals were in grave danger of extinction. They convinced many of the world's governments of the same thing, and the law banning the sale of ivory was passed.[1]

▲ *When a female elephant is killed, its orphaned calves are often forced to fend for themselves. A national park near Nairobi, Kenya, has an elephant orphanage. This orphanage worker, Bernard Kilonzo, is feeding one of the orphans.*

The land used by growing human populations has taken away the elephants' much needed wildlife space. The threat from poachers is constant. Environmentalists are hoping that long-range studies and research will give people the information they need to start saving the elephants. These studies will track such important information as elephant birthrates, death rates, how far they travel for food, and what their nutritional needs are.

## ▶ Reasons to Save the Elephants

These scientists are also working hard at proving that elephants are very sophisticated and complex animals. It is thought that these animals form lifelong friendships, celebrate births, and mourn, or feel sad, when their elephant friends die. The scientists are hoping that this information will make people care about elephants and make them want to work at saving them.

In addition to the critical information that the researchers are finding in the field, they also play a much more obvious role in protecting the elephants. Poachers will not try to kill elephants if there is a researcher in the area studying the elephants. Having someone in the area can be crucial to the elephants' survival.

When poachers kill a female elephant, it means a lot more than just one less elephant in the herd. Male orphaned elephants are more likely to leave the group at a younger age, which means they are subjected to danger. Female elephants who grow up without mothers are usually not good mothers themselves. It simply changes the entire family unit.

## ▷ Getting Governments to Help

Another problem is that even states, or countries, in Africa that are working to protect the elephant often do not agree with each other. They have different totals for the number of elephants that are in the wild. This is extremely harmful because the public is not always sure how severe the shortage of elephants is. Conservation, or saving the elephant, really depends on public opinion. It is important for the public to have the right information. Conservationists rely on raising money from the public, and they also count on the public to write letters to politicians and other influential people to help. If the public is confused, then those efforts may die as well.

🔺 *An African elephant calf and its mother. In 1998, many protested when the South African government captured young elephants and sold them to zoos. It was alleged that the baby elephants were mistreated.*

## ▷ Economy vs. Environment

Economies of some African countries are very poor. Governments and business owners are looking to make money. Some African countries have taken advantage of an "educational" law that allows them to capture baby elephants and sell them to zoos and circuses around the world. In 1998, there was international outrage after it was discovered that the South African government had captured and taken many baby elephants away from their families and then sent the animals to training facilities that critics said were too harsh for the animals. An animal cruelty case was tried in a court of law, and many of the animals were finally returned to the wild. Some, however, were sold to zoos in China, Sweden, and Germany.[2]

The international ban on trading endangered animals means that organizations are supposed to check first to make sure that these zoos and circuses can treat the animals well. However, they are usually short on staff and so backed up with work that they can not check to see if the zoos will make a good home before the animals are shipped there.

## Dangers

As you can see, the elephants face growing challenges from many very different places. They face danger from poachers looking to make money by selling their ivory. They face danger from conflict with humans as more and more forestland gets used up by growing populations. They also face danger from countries looking to fill their zoos and circuses with elephants. The bottom line is that it is all about money. It remains to be seen if the elephants can survive the greed of some groups of people.

# Will the Elephant Survive?

The best thing going for the African elephant right now is that people are talking and writing about them. Countries are meeting and discussing how to save these wondrous creatures. It seems that the majority of the world realizes that driving the elephants to extinction would be a terrible mistake.

## ▷ Government Help

In April 2003, the African nation of Ghana hosted a two-day meeting of a group called MIKE. This stands for Monitoring the Illegal Killing of Elephants. Representatives came from many countries throughout Africa and Asia. Their goal was a simple one: long-term management of elephant populations.

Meetings like this try to show other people how valuable the elephant is. They stress how forest elephants are the only animals large enough to eat and then spread certain seeds of plants to help them grow. Some of the experts say that without elephants about 30 percent of the different types of trees in the forest would disappear.

They also argue that without elephants Africa would lose its grasslands or savannas. That would mean that all the types of animals that live in the savannas, like giraffes, zebras, and lions, would have to adapt to new and different types of places to live. The theory behind this is that without elephants, the grasslands would become overgrown with woody plants and become more of a forest. Animals would start to vanish because the forest cannot support the same types of animals as the wide-open plains.

▲ Many countries and environmental groups are working to ensure the safety of elephants such as these.

## ▷ Environmental Groups

Aside from governments, there are many environmental groups that are working hard to make sure elephants survive. One of these groups, LWE, or Living With Elephants, likes to reach out to children—among other groups—to teach them about elephants. The organization hosts groups of children and has them interact personally with real elephants. The idea is that if children learn to love and admire elephants, then the children will do things to protect them when they are grown.

Some countries have even tried extreme measures to try and make sure the elephants are safe. The African

country of Botswana has electrified a portion of fence to try to keep the elephants from wandering too close to where man lives. Some say elephants will get nervous because of the electric fences, and it will cause more problems as they try to escape their enclosed habitats.[1]

## ▶ Sad Facts

While some countries continue to work to protect elephant herds, the sad truth is that these animals have vanished from several African countries. The governments of these countries either wanted to make a profit from selling ivory, or civil war and poverty made saving the elephants a low priority.

Biologist and elephant researcher Cynthia Moss has lived with elephants in Africa for more than two decades.

▲ This herd of elephants is taking a drink. Elephants have disappeared from many places in Africa where they had once been native.

An African elephant rubs its trunk against a tree. Elephants use their trunks to recognize the shape of objects and whether they are hot or cold.

She has seen elephant populations dwindle or simply vanish from certain countries. Her research found that the country of Chad had fifteen thousand elephants before a civil war broke out. There were less than two thousand after the war was over. She also found that in the country of Sudan, wild gangs of poachers armed with automatic rifles wiped out every elephant in the country to get and sell the ivory. In Somalia, aerial photographs capture more images of dead elephants than they do of live ones.

"The situation is depressing but it may not be irreversible," Moss writes in her book *Elephant Memories*. "There are people working very hard to halt the downward trend."[2] That statement was made in 1988. That is how long the elephants have been in extreme danger.

## ▷ Comeback

The worldwide ban on the ivory trade went into effect in 1990, and elephants have begun to make a comeback. The elephants are starting to repopulate herds as countries try to balance man's needs with elephants' needs. They have to come to some conclusions regarding land and space. Yet there is still the question of ivory.

Should countries be able to sell the ivory of elephants that die naturally? Will this hurt conservation efforts? What about culling, or killing, elephants legally for their ivory once populations reach a certain level? These are all questions that conservation groups and independent governments disagree on. Even the United States, which supports conservation of elephants, is not sure where to stand on certain issues. For example, people in a poor country banned from selling ivory obtained legally may resort to selling illegal drugs to make up for the lost money.

In particular, the countries of Zimbabwe, Botswana, and Namibia have repeatedly asked for permission to sell existing ivory and to start killing elephants in populated areas.

## Crucial to Conserve

It appears as if enough people have started caring about the future of the African elephant for it to ensure future genera-tions will be able to enjoy the magnificent creatures as we do. Most American zoos and nature museums today take the time to point out endangered animals, what a loss it would

▲ This storeroom in South Africa has a stockpile of ivory. South Africa, Botswana, Namibia, Zambia, and Zimbabwe would like to be able to sell the ivory they have confiscated from poachers. Selling the ivory, they say, would help the economy of these nations.

▲ *Elephants are majestic animals that many people enjoy going to see at national parks, on safaris, and at zoos. Hopefully, governments and people can work together to save these animals.*

be if they became extinct, and how we can support groups that are trying to save them. It is crucial that conservation efforts stay strong, well funded, and focused. After all, it takes an elephant twenty-two months—almost two years— to have a baby elephant. That means it takes many years for elephants to repopulate herds once they have disappeared. Let us hope we never have to face that possibility.

This series is based on the Endangered and Threatened Wildlife
list compiled by the U.S. Fish and Wildlife Service (USFWS).
Each book explores an endangered or threatened animal, tells
why it has become endangered or threatened, and explains the
efforts being made to restore the species' population.

*The United States Fish and Wildlife Service, in the
Department of the Interior, and the National Marine Fisheries
Service, in the Department of Commerce, share responsibility for
administration of the Endangered Species Act.*

*In 1973, Congress took the farsighted step of creating the
Endangered Species Act, widely regarded as the world's strongest
and most effective wildlife conservation law. It set an ambitious
goal: to reverse the alarming trend of human-caused extinction
that threatened the ecosystems we all share.*

The complete list of Endangered and Threatened
Wildlife and Plants can be found at
**http://endangered.fws.gov/wildlife.html#Species**.

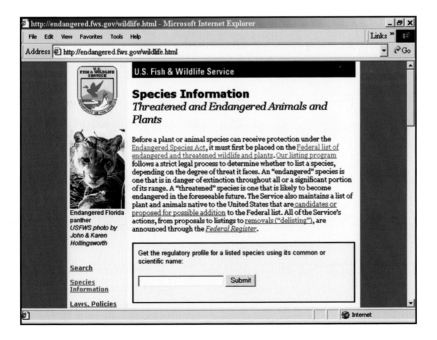

## Chapter 1. An Illegal Slaughter

1. Karen de Seve, "The Poaching Problem," *Nature: The Elephants of Africa*, 2001, <http://www.pbs.org/wnet/nature/elephants/poaching.html> (March 5, 2004).

## Chapter 2. Special Characteristics

1. Karen de Seve, "Life of an Elephant," *Nature: The Elephants of Africa*, 2001, <http://www.pbs.org/wnet/nature/elephants/life.html> (March 5, 2004).

## Chapter 4. Growing Concern

1. Riverdeep Interactive Learning Limited, "The Ivory Ban," *Riverdeep*, 2004, <http://www.riverdeep.net/current/2000/05/front.110500.ivory.jhtml> (February 18, 2004).

2. Adam Roberts, "Botswana's Baby Elephants Saved from International Trade," *Botswana*, n.d., <http://www.awionline.org/wildlife/tuli.html> (February 18, 2004).

## Chapter 5. Will the Elephant Survive?

1. J. G. Du Toit, "Introduction of Family Groups on Game Ranches and Reserves (RSA)," *Information about Game (A – L)*, 2001, <http://bigfive.jl.co.za/family_groups.htm> (February 18, 2004).

2. Cynthia Moss, *Elephant Memories* (New York: Ballantine Books, 1988), p. 296.

## Further Reading

Dudley, William. *Africa.* Farmington Hills, Mich.: Gale Group, 2000.

James, Ellen Foley. *Little Bull: Growing up in Africa's Elephant Kingdom.* New York: Sterling Publishers, 1998.

Levine, Stuart P. *The Elephant.* Farmington Hills, Mich.: Gale Group, 1998.

Pringle, Laurence. *Elephant Woman: Cynthia Moss Explores the World of Elephants.* New York: Atheneum Books, 1997.

Schlaepfer, Gloria G. *Elephants.* Tarrytown, N.Y.: Benchmark Books, 2003.

Schwabacher, Martin. *Elephants.* Tarrytown, N.Y.: Marshall Cavendish, 2001.

Smith, Roland. *African Elephants.* Minneapolis, Minn.: Lerner Publications, 1995.

Smith, Roland and Michael J. Schmidt. *In the Forest With Elephants.* San Diego, Calif.: Harcourt Children's Books, 1998.

Sobol, Richard. *One More Elephant: The Fight to Save Wildlife in Uganda.* New York: Cobblehill Books, 1995.

Stone, Tanya. *Elephants.* Farmington Hills, Mich.: Gale Group, 2003.

Weintraub, Aileen. *Discovering Africa's Land, People, and Wildlife.* Berkeley Heights, N.J.: Enslow Publishers, Inc., 2004.